Original title:
The Grapefruit's Reflection

Copyright © 2025 Creative Arts Management OÜ
All rights reserved.

Author: William Hawthorne
ISBN HARDBACK: 978-1-80586-393-9
ISBN PAPERBACK: 978-1-80586-865-1

## Jigsaw of Juicy Reflections

In the morning sun, oh what a sight,
A citrus orb, so round and bright.
With a wink and a giggle, it rolls on the floor,
Creating a mess, who could ask for more?

Peeling away layers, it's quite the affair,
Juice squirts out, splatting everywhere.
With each tasty section, laughter ensues,
A playful dance of citrus hues.

On the table it wobbles, a jester in fruit,
With seeds for the audience, not one will dispute.
It teases the spoons, and hops with glee,
"Oh look at me, I'm as funny as a bee!"

As I take a slice, it grins at my face,
A zestful surprise, a juicy embrace.
With every sweet bite, joy spreads like cheer,
Oh what a wonder this fruit holds dear!

## Citrus Under Moonlight

Under the glow of moonlit skies,
Oranges wink with mischievous eyes.
Lemons giggle in the silver light,
As limes join in a playful fight.

They dance around in citrus glee,
Spinning stories, wild and free.
With each twist and silly slip,
They jostle in their fruity trip.

## **Brightness and Bitterness**

In a world of sweet and sour,
Lemons plot their tartest power.
They laugh when sweetness takes a spill,
As grapefruits chase their bitter thrill.

With pep and zest they tease and jest,
A fruit salad's oddball quest.
For in the bowl where flavors clash,
Each citrus laughs, goes bold, and brash.

**Juxtaposed Flavors**


Citrus kin, a wild parade,
Brighter shades, but not dismayed.
Tartness bows to sweetness here,
While oranges belt their citrus cheer.

A challenge thrown, a lime's sly grin,
Mango's sweet, but who will win?
The mix of doubts and playful fears,
Brought together through citrus cheers!

**The Charmed Citrus**

In a kitchen where dreams unfold,
A charmed fruit rests, fierce and bold.
With peels like armor, shining bright,
It casts a spell beneath the light.

Lemonade streams from every twist,
A bubbling wish that can't be missed.
The zestful magic that they sow,
Turns every meal into a show.

## Fragments of Morning Light

In morning glow, a slice resides,
A sprightly grin, where sweetness hides.
With a wink it waits, all plump and round,
In citrus tales, laughter is found.

A fork in hand, I take a bite,
Zesty giggles burst with delight.
As juice escapes, a playful dance,
Who knew breakfast could enhance the chance?

## **Bitter Sweetness in Glass**

In a crystal cup, sunshine twirls,
Bitter and sweet in citrus swirls.
Like a joker masked in zestful glee,
Sips bring chuckles, try one, you'll see!

Each drop a jester, playful and bright,
Making faces, it's pure delight.
In every sip, a laugh takes flight,
Bitter moments feel just right.

## Juicy Mirages

Underneath the sun's warm grasp,
Wobbly blobs in the summer's clasp.
Mirages dance with sugary grace,
Who knew splashes could misplace taste?

Each splash a giggle, each taste a jest,
Dreaming of fruit, it's simply the best.
Juicy mirages that tease the tongue,
Making each morning feel ever young.

## **Blossoms in Transparent Waters**

In clear reflections, blossoms bloom,
Floating fruit in a playful room.
Each petal held in watery cheer,
Whispers of laughter ring in the air.

Waves of humor swirl all around,
Bubbles find joy as they bounce off the ground.
Sip by sip, the giggles grow,
Who knew nature loved a show?

## **Reflective Haven**

In a bowl, a bright sphere sits,
With a grin, it smiles and flits.
Juicy thoughts on the surface gleam,
A citrus dream, oh what a theme.

It bounces on the counter's edge,
Wobbling like a jolly pledge.
Peeling layers with a twist of fun,
Squirting giggles in the sun.

Each slice reveals a vibrant hue,
Like little hats, a zesty crew.
Witty seeds, they dance and play,
In this sunny, silly ballet.

So grab a spoon, let's dig right in,
Taste the laughter, feel the spin.
A burst of zest, a cheerful cheer,
In this reflective atmosphere.

## Essence of a Morning Solstice

Morning light spills all around,
A citrus ball, our joy unbound.
Sliced with glee, the colors burst,
Bitter laughs quenched with sweet thirst.

A breakfast king in a sunny throne,
Crown of pith, seeds brightly shone.
Rolling on the kitchen floor,
It begs for juice, but wants much more.

Pitted thoughts with peels a-twirl,
Each wedge a giggle, give it a whirl.
Spilling tangy tales of yore,
In the morning sun, we all adore.

So let's toast to this zesty joke,
A citrus laugh, a sly little poke.
In every slice, a giggle found,
The essence of joy in flavors round.

**Citrus Reverie**

In the fridge, a treasure waits,
Juicy orb with fun debates.
Peeling back the tangy skin,
Oh, what madness lies within!

With each wedge, a grin expands,
Citrus giggles in our hands.
Spritz of juice in the morning air,
A zesty dance, without a care.

Sweet and sour, a playful clash,
With every bite, a vibrant splash.
A laughing fruit on a sunny plate,
Join the feast, don't be late!

So here's to joy in every round,
Let's make a toast to funny sound.
In every bite, a jubilant spree,
Citrus dreams for you and me.

## **Echoes of Sunlit Flesh**

Beneath the sun, a citrus glow,
With each slice, the laughter flows.
Echoes of juice in the air,
A zesty fruit, without a care.

Like a clown in a fruity suit,
With pithy jokes, it's rather cute.
Rolling round the morning cheer,
Who knew we'd end up here, my dear?

With every peel, a story told,
Of sunlit days and joys unfold.
Seeds scatter laughter, seeds of fun,
Chasing shadows 'til the day is done.

So let's rejoice in this fruity jest,
A tapestry of zest and zest.
In echoes bright, we find the glee,
A sunlit feast for you and me.

## Zest of a Thousand Days

In the morning light, so bright and round,
A citrus gem, in laughter found.
Its tangy laugh, a pucker so bold,
Beneath the sun, tales of zest untold.

With every slice, a splash, a cheer,
Juices dance, oh so near.
A breakfast riot, with colors galore,
Who knew fruit could start a roar?

Glancing back, the mirror shows,
A citrus grin, as sweetness flows.
Oh, what a day it promises to be,
With zesty joy, so wild and free.

From tangy bites to giggling spills,
A bowl of sunshine, laughter fills.
Each segment sings a jolly tune,
Unraveling woes like a bright balloon.

## Shattered Citrus Dreams

Once in a bowl, bright dreams did lay,
A citrus kingdom, in wild dismay.
With one small tumble, oh what a sight,
Segments flying, in sheer delight!

A splat on the floor, juice takes the lead,
Citrus laughter, a zesty creed.
What fun it is to watch them play,
In a daring dance, they rolled away.

With every bounce, joy fills the room,
These shattered dreams, with zest they bloom.
No longer whole, yet sweetness remains,
In fragments bright, hilarity reigns.

So here's to the mess, and chaos, too,
When life gives you slices, dance like goo.
For in the spills and the dreams undone,
Citrus giggles have just begun!

## **Flavors of Daybreak**

Awake to flavors, the sun's warm kiss,
Bright citrus notes you cannot miss.
Morning joy in a bowl set right,
Unraveling bubble of pure delight.

Sipping zest from a happy cup,
With each tang, you just can't give up.
The flavors burst, in a playful spree,
Who knew breakfast could be so free?

Dancing slices twirl around,
In the bowl, they leap and bound.
A wink from the fruit, a wink from me,
In a citrus ball, we're filled with glee.

Laughing toward another day,
With fruity dreams, let's laugh and play.
For every bite, like sunshine spreads,
We're savoring life in citrus threads.

## Radiance in the Bowl

In the heart of the kitchen, a bowl shines bright,
Citrus glory, a comical sight.
A radiant orb, with laughs to lend,
In segments ripe, the fun won't end.

Yellow and pink, a palette's delight,
Juicy jokes that burst and excite.
A silly dance, a giggle parade,
With each little slice, memories made.

As morning unfolds with innocent cheer,
Citrus whispers, come near, come near!
To taste the laughter, what a fine goal,
In this charming bowl, we nourish the soul.

So gather around, let the good times roll,
With every bright bite, we're freckled and whole.
In radiant zest, our spirits take flight,
With fruit's funny glow, we dance with delight.

## Exploring Juicy Horizons

In a world that's oft so bright,
Citrus balance brings delight.
With every slice a secret shown,
Juicy laughter, all alone.

Peeling back the zesty skin,
A splash of fun, let's dive right in!
With every wedge, joy does unfold,
A treasure trove of tales retold.

Bouncing bubbles fill the air,
Each segment's giggle sparks a flare.
We twirl and dance on sunny days,
In citrus joy, our heart sways.

Oh, the stories that we share,
With frothy drinks, we conquer care.
Exploring realms of flavor bold,
Where every laugh is worth its weight in gold.

## Reflections in Amber Tides

In a bowl of amber cheer,
Waves of zest wash up quite near.
Floating dreams in citrus brine,
Giggling fruit, a sweet design.

As I sip my tangy brew,
Thoughts of laughter come anew.
With every splash, our troubles cease,
In this pool, we find our peace.

Funny faces, peels galore,
Make us chuckle, ask for more.
Juggling slices, what a sight,
Bright reflections, pure delight.

In the juice, we find our muse,
With every wedge, we set to cruise.
Amber waves, a tangy rhyme,
Moments shared, lost in time.

## Secrets of the Zesty Realm

In the land of zesty schemes,
Citrus laughter fills our dreams.
Frothy drinks, a bubbling tune,
Dancing flavors, afternoon.

Ponder not the bitter days,
Swirling sweetness on the rays.
We've tamed the tart, embraced the fun,
In this realm, we're never done.

Secrets hidden in each bite,
Sharing smiles, a pure delight.
I'll squeeze a joke, you'll lick a face,
With zesty joy, we find our place.

Here, the sun will always shine,
Every fruit tells tales divine.
Together in this whimsy space,
Laughter echoes, we embrace.

## Mornings in Citrus Shades

In the morn, the sun does gleam,
Citrus hues, a waking dream.
Toast adorned with shining zest,
Every bite's a quirky quest.

Sipping juice in laughter's glow,
Wakey-wakey, let's start the show.
With tangy smiles to greet the day,
In citrus shades, we dance and play.

Fruits in bowls begin to twirl,
Brightest colors dance and swirl.
Bananas sing while lemons jive,
In this morning, we come alive.

Joyful moments, bright and sweet,
Citrus laughter, can't be beat.
Every sunrise brings the chance,
To embrace this fruity dance.

## **Colors in the Reflective Pool**

Bouncing bright hues on the water,
A yellow ball, oh what a totter!
Green bounce here, and red rolls there,
Watch out for splashes, if you dare!

Pink polka dots, they wiggle and sway,
In this silly game, no serious play.
Chasing rainbows that just won't stay,
Giggles echo, come join the fray!

Mirrors of laughter, each wave a grin,
Reflections dancing, let the fun begin.
With each bounce, a surprise in store,
Colors collide, who could ask for more?

Sunny hues in the pool so wide,
Swirling and twirling, they can't hide.
Oh what a sight, what a hullabaloo!
Join in the chaos, there's fun for you!

## Dancing in Sunlit Echoes

Sunbeams twirl, oh what a sight,
Dancing shadows, feeling just right.
Lemon drops pirouette with glee,
While orange slices join the spree.

Bananas break into silly jives,
As laughter flares, the whole world thrives.
Bouncing beats, and giggles galore,
Dancing in echoes, who could ask for more?

Grapes prance on the grass so bright,
Under blue skies, pure delight.
With each step, a mischief anew,
Join the fun, let your spirit imbue!

In this sunny sway, joy comes alive,
Skip and hop, let your heart thrive.
Every moment, a joyous addition,
In this dance, we find our mission!

## The Essence of Forgotten Summers

Whispers of days in the warm sun's glow,
Sticky fingers from treats we know.
Sandcastle dreams and laughter loud,
Memories made, so bright, so proud.

Splashing in pools, a cannonball show,
Floating by, where wild wildflowers grow.
Exotic scents waft on the breeze,
Sunny mischief among the trees.

Pickle juice sips from a colorful cup,
Flip-flops flying as we jump up.
Oh, for those days, we'd giggle and cheer,
With each sunny laugh, summer's clear.

But as we age, we still reminisce,
In every laugh, a fleeting bliss.
Savor the moments, let joy resound,
In forgotten summers, pure gold is found!

## **Shades of Zesty Harmony**

In a world where zesty flavors play,
Lemon-lime jokes crack us each day.
Sour meets sweet, a wonderful twist,
Combining our laughter, none can resist.

Juicy puns as ripe as can be,
In this zesty realm, we all agree.
Spicy whispers and dandy delights,
Creating a blend of whimsical sights.

The tangy tunes of citrus croons,
Brightening nights with fruitful tunes.
Songs of laughter, in tones so unique,
Join the chorus, let joy sneak!

Oh, the harmony found in fruit's delight,
Zest brings us together, shining so bright.
With a wink and a grin, let flavors flow,
In this world of fun, we steal the show!

## Citrus Echoes

A fruit so bright and round,
It rolls on the kitchen floor.
Chasing it around, I found,
It giggled from the back door.

In a bowl with apples and pears,
It claimed it had a zesty laugh.
But when I tried to share my cares,
It squirted juice like a silly gaff.

Orange sun with a hint of cheer,
Whisper jokes to the morning air.
The zestiness spreads far and near,
As fruit flies dance without a care.

With every slice, a chuckle grows,
As I wipe juice off my face.
Who knew a fruit could be so prose,
In this zany kitchen race?

## Sunrise in a Zest

Awake to a citrus smile,
With sunshine poured like juice.
I slice and serve with style,
As laughter takes the truce.

The toast adorned with yellow spread,
I toast my grapefruit slice.
It winks at me, no words unsaid,
This breakfast is precise!

Thoughts bubble up like fizzy drinks,
As spoons clink in pure delight.
A fallout of juicy jests and winks,
Let's savor the morning light!

I dance around the kitchen floor,
To tunes the fruit proclaimed.
In zest and fun, I can't ignore,
This crazy life we tamed!

## Juicy Shadows

In the fridge, a secret waits,
Shadows shaped like silly smiles.
Each one dreams of grapefruit fates,
And dances in fruity styles.

Underneath the kitchen lights,
They plot a plot of laughter loud.
To prank the eaters in their sights,
This fruit that's mighty, proud.

With a toss, they leap and roll,
Making mischief every day.
Who knew a citrus could control,
The fun in such a playful way?

At the picnic, they reveal,
A joke to make us all burst out.
A juicy laugh, a sweet appeal,
These shadows are what life's about!

## **Fragrant Light**

A whiff of citrus fills the air,
As morning rays peek through.
It tickles noses, without a care,
And gets each giggle anew.

The zest of life, in every peel,
Sprinkles chuckles on the floor.
What's the secret in its feel?
A scent that opens every door.

At nighttime, it glows with cheer,
Sending aromas to the stars.
With every laugh, it draws us near,
Enthralled like bouncy cars.

So slice away the midnight slice,
Let laughter pour like golden light.
In fragrant fun, let's roll the dice,
And treasure joy beyond the night!

## A Slice Beneath the Surface

In a fruit bowl, bright and round,
A secret giggle can be found.
With each bite, the juice does splatter,
And sticky fingers? Oh, what a matter!

It claims to be so healthy and fine,
But leaves us bold, like citrus wine.
We laugh at juice stains on our shirts,
And in the kitchen, chaos flirts.

The pith is soft, a sponge of cheer,
Zesty jokes that bring us near.
With every wedge, a joke's reprise,
Sour faces turn into sweet surprise!

So here's a toast to our sunny friend,
Whose flavor dances, never ends.
We'll savor each slice as if it's fate,
With laughter stuffed upon our plate!

## The Juiciest Musings

In morning sun, a zesty thought,
What's juicier than never caught?
Rinds may wrinkle, but can't disguise,
The giggles found in each surprise.

Pulp parties, they're quite the show,
With citrus hats that steal the glow.
We squeeze the jokes like juice on toast,
And laugh aloud, with zest, we boast!

Each segment bursts with flavored fun,
Like fizzy drinks on the run.
So let's devour this tangy treat,
And dance on tongues with citrus beat!

For life's too short to simply bite,
Let's share some laughter, pure delight.
With every taste, a playful wink,
Sweet-sour musings, let's not shrink!

## Citrus Nectar Tales

A story starts with a citrus peel,
Whispering secrets in a fruity wheel.
The juice is bold, the smile's bright,
It tickles our sides with pure delight.

In a blender, chaos soon begins,
As laughter swirls with fruity spins.
Flavors collide like old-time friends,
Creating mess where the fun never ends!

Each splash is like a playful quirk,
That makes us grin, makes laughter lurk.
As we sip tales of tangy bliss,
We can't resist a citrus kiss!

So raise your glass, toast to the zest,
Life's sweetest moments, surely the best.
With every drink, let laughter sail,
In the realm of citrus, we shall prevail!

## **Luminous Layers**

Peeling back layers, what do we find?
Bright laughs and puns that twist the mind.
In every bite, a giggle hides,
Citrus charm that tickles sides.

Juicy whispers fill the air,
Who knew fruit could so much share?
We slice and dice, the party's on,
With every wedge, our worries gone.

Underneath that zesty skin,
Lies a laughter that won't give in.
A playful mess, oh what a sight,
As juice dribbles down, we feel so light!

So take a slice, and let it glow,
In citrus realms, the fun will flow.
With every munch, we cheer and play,
Luminous layers, brightening our day!

## **Vibrant Echoes of Citrus**

In the bowl sat a sphere, so bright,
A zesty orb, a delight in sight.
Giggling at the spoon's silly dance,
It splattered juice, oh what a chance!

A yellow grin, it wore so proud,
Squeezed by hands that cheered out loud.
The juice shot forth, a citrus spray,
Who knew fruit could cause such play?

With each slice, they giggled and hummed,
As pulp and pith together bummed.
A tasty prank on those who miss,
The joys of zest in fruity bliss!

So here's to the fruit with the brightest hue,
Whose laughter bursts with each gooey boo.
Let's squeeze out joy from peels so bright,
Citrus giggles from morning till night.

## Dance of the Citrus Spirit

In a kitchen bright with morning light,
An orb of fun takes a joyful flight.
It rolls away, oh what a tease,
Dodging the hands that dare to squeeze!

With a twist and a spin, it jumps and jives,
The dance of zest, where humor thrives.
It spins in chaos, and laughs abound,
A citrus fiesta, where bliss is found!

With each slice, a giggle escapes,
The tangy laughter slips through the grapes.
Its essence burst, oh what a clamor,
Creating laughs like a comic banner!

So let's toast to this fruity bard,
Who brings us joy, though slipping's hard.
A citrus cheer in every bite,
Fun and laughter from morning til night!

**Clarity of Golden Essence**

A fruit so bright, it caught my eye,
Golden hue like sunshine in the sky.
With a squirt and a giggle, a twist of fate,
This playful orb can't help but celebrate!

It sits with grace, a golden dome,
In every slice, it calls me home.
Pulp and juice like laughter spills,
In every bite, it gives me thrills!

The rind, so bright, a jester's cap,
It rolls around, no time for a nap.
With each juice droplet, laughter ensues,
A citrus spirit that can't refuse!

Here's to the fruit of giggles and glee,
Nature's jest with endless spree.
So grab a spoon, let's make some zest,
For joy and laughter, it's simply the best!

## Tapestry of Tangy Bliss

In a patch of sunshine, a fruit sways light,
Golden orb, oh what a sight!
A zany slice, what a curious peel,
Creating laughter with each juicy meal!

As I cut through, it gives a wink,
The juice bursts out, and I can't help but think.
Giggles echo, with every chop,
This citrus prankster, it just won't stop!

With a tangy grin, it cheers me on,
In every bite, the frown is gone.
A splash of sweetness in this crazy mix,
Turning dull days into citrus tricks!

So here's to the zest that brings us cheer,
A tapestry of laughs, oh so near.
Let's savor the moment, let laughter grow,
With a fruity friend, let the joy overflow!

## Fruitful Contemplations

In the bowl sits bright and round,
Winking at me without a sound.
Did you know, it's a jester bold,
With tangy tales yet to be told?

Peeling back skin, what a delight,
A burst of laughter, oh what a sight!
Zesty giggles dance on my tongue,
As fruity puns are freshly sung.

Squeeze my brain, I'm in a squeeze,
As I ponder such fruity bees.
Juicy jokes fill the kitchen air,
Making me grin and do a dare!

So here's to fun, let's celebrate,
Slicing sweetness on my plate.
A citrus clown, my fruity friend,
Brings a chuckle till the end.

## **Echoes of Sweetness**

A citrus ball with a cheeky grin,
Bounces around, let the laughter begin!
Juicy secrets wait to be shared,
In this bright orb, nothing's spared.

Bright bursts of flavor, a zesty laugh,
Sliced and served, oh what a craft!
Every bite brings a smile so wide,
Funny faces this fruit will provide.

With every juice that trickles down,
Comes a giggle, never a frown.
Sour and sweet, a comic twist,
A fruit so bold, it can't be missed.

Chasing laughs like it's a game,
In my bowl, it's never the same.
Each time I bite, I'm in a trance,
In the rhythm of a fruity dance.

## Radiant Juices

Sunlight trapped in a zesty skin,
It giggles and glows, what a win!
Squeezed so bright, it laughs with flair,
Splashes of joy dance in the air.

Whispering jokes behind a peel,
Tickling taste buds, what a deal!
Rind on the outside, fun to bite,
It keeps on teasing, pure delight.

Pulp so playful, bouncing around,
With every slice, there's laughter found.
A vibrant jest in each segment,
In this fruit world, I'm the president!

Bring on the smiles, let's juice it up,
Turning life into a laughing cup.
With citrus charm, we'll take a ride,
Juicy joy that's hard to hide.

## **Refractions of a Sunlit Orb**

Behold this orb, a trickster's design,
Reflecting sunlight like fine wine.
A playful wink with every slice,
Sweetness masked in zesty vice.

A jolt of laughter with every zest,
Tickles my senses, oh what a jest!
Colors burst as I take a bite,
Juicy giggles, pure delight.

In a fruit bowl, chaos reigns,
With slices sparking funny pains.
Its laughter echoes, bounces loud,
Bringing joy to every crowd.

So let us cheer with every drop,
This sunlit orb will never stop.
With fruity fun, we'll make a scene,
In this zest-filled, cheerful sheen.

## The Bitter-Sweet Mirage

In the bowl, a fruit so bright,
A citrus ball, a funny sight.
Juicy tales in every slice,
Bringing laughter, oh so nice.

With a grin, it flaunts its zest,
Puckered lips, it's not like rest.
Fruits can't giggle, yet they thrive,
In our smiles, they feel alive.

Peel it back, the scent escapes,
Dancing kids in citrus capes.
Every bite, a story spun,
Who knew fruit could be such fun?

So let's toast with juice so bright,
For fruity moments, pure delight.
Laughter mixed with every taste,
A Mirage we will not waste.

## Slices of Serenity

A sunny orb upon the plate,
Slices smiling, isn't that great?
The tangy bite that starts the show,
Jokes unfold as juices flow.

Not a battle but a game,
Squeeze it gently, what a claim!
With every slice, a burst of cheer,
Turn that frown into a leer.

Pulp and zest in harmony,
Bouncing flavors, wild and free.
In each wedge, a giggly tone,
A happiness we can't disown.

So gather round, let's share each bite,
Turn the ordinary into bright.
A bowl of joy that melts away,
Slices sing, and we just play.

**Citrus Dreams Unfold**

In the morning, sunlight wakes,
Citrus scents, our laughter takes.
Yellow, pink, a playful tease,
Dreaming sweetly, with such ease.

Juicy joys that wobble 'round,
Silly faces, laughter found.
Pulp and puns, a funny dance,
Every bite, a goofy chance.

Peeling back the layers thin,
Each slice whispers where we've been.
Sour giggles, sweet delight,
In this dream, all feels just right.

Join the fun, let funny rise,
In this fruit, a bright surprise.
Citrus tales forever told,
In this laughter, dreams unfold.

## A Tangy Reverie

Once upon a bright delight,
Sliced and diced, what a fright!
A citrus tale, so tangy-sweet,
Every segment, a comic treat.

With a squirt, the giggle flies,
Waving zest beneath the skies.
Poking fun with every peel,
Lemon's cousin has a feel!

Juicy squabbles on my plate,
Jokes collide, isn't that great?
Laughter flows like rich, thick juice,
In this world, we can't let loose.

So join this tangy reverie,
Laughs and bites, what joy to see!
Citrus giggles, bright and bold,
In each moment, stories told.

## **Tangy Shadows**

In the kitchen light, a fruit lies still,
Swaying gently, without any will.
It spins and rolls, with zest in sight,
A citrus dance, oh what a delight!

Lemonade dreams and orange hopes,
Pulpular gossip, as it gropes.
With every slice, its laughter spills,
Juicy tales, oh, what a thrill!

A peel of laughter, a zesty smile,
Bright colored fruit, with a hint of guile.
In a salad bowl, it plots and schemes,
A citrus caper, just like our dreams.

When served with pride, it makes a jest,
In a fruit party, it's surely the best!
With zingers and zests, it steals the show,
A twist in every bite, a berry glow!

## Sun-Kissed Whispers

In the orchard light, a ball of cheer,
Whispers of sunshine are drawing near.
With every squirt, a giggle erupts,
A juicy clown, all sweetness and cups!

It winks at the lime, then gives a nudge,
Together they're bright, they hardly judge.
Peeling back laughter, the fun unfolds,
A zesty friendship, as each story's told.

With every sip of citrusy grace,
A spritz of humor fills the space.
The fruit bowl dances, swirling around,
In fruity banter, joy can be found.

Sunlit humor in every zest,
Peeling away sadness, that's its quest!
In bright citrus hues, life finds its way,
With every giggle, we seize the day!

## Orb of Juicy Secrets

Underneath the sun, a glob delights,
Sharing gossip with the stars at nights.
A citrus orb with secrets galore,
Exudes a punchline, begging for more!

In a smoothie glass, it blends and swirls,
Transforming into laughter, as it twirls.
With every scoop, a tickle feels right,
A fruity jest, oh what a sight!

Peeling layers, its stories unwind,
Juicy secrets that are hard to find.
With each drop, a chuckle escapes,
A tangy giggle that brightly shapes!

Amidst the leaves where flavors collide,
The orb shares its jest, with endless pride.
In a world of fruit, it's the comedic king,
A punchy laugh, with every zing!

**Crystal Reflections**

In the morning light, it sits so grand,
Reflecting tales that no one planned.
With a citrus grin, it gleams with charm,
Even a kitchen knife couldn't cause harm!

Every slice reveals the fun within,
A juicy secret that makes us grin.
With a squirt and a splash, it has its way,
Turning lunch hour into a playful fray!

In the bowl of fruit, it holds court strong,
Its sweet little antics, can't be wrong.
With laughs and giggles, it takes a stand,
A fruity jester, life unplanned!

Reflecting laughter in each juicy bite,
Sparkling humor in the afternoon light.
Come join the fun, let the taste collide,
In food and laughter, we'll joyfully ride!

## **Aroma in Twilight**

In twilight's glow, a scent so bright,
A hazy orb, a citrus delight.
Squirrels gather, curious orbs in tow,
Laughing at what they think they know.

Essence dances, sweet and bold,
A modest fruit with tales untold.
Under the moon, they take a chance,
Rolling around in a silly dance.

A burst of zest in a feathery breeze,
Unruly laughter among the trees.
A creature sneezes, and what a sight!
As segments tumble in pure delight.

They giggle soft, the stars poke fun,
At fruity foes, their jests weigh a ton.
Flavors clash, a tangy dispute,
In twilight's embrace, they all stay cute.

## Sweet Sap from Above

From the branches high, a sweet sap drips,
A sticky trickle, it playfully slips.
Bees toss and turn, in sticky flights,
Bumping and bouncing in cheerful bites.

A flavor burst, nature's candy prize,
Bringing sneezes, and no surprise.
Juicy tidbits, a slapstick show,
Nature's own circus, with smiles aglow.

Dancing ants form a wriggly line,
Chasing drops that taste divine.
Slurping sounds as they dive in,
A comedy sketch where no one can win.

A gathering grand, oh what a scene,
Fruitful laughter, where joy is keen.
As shadows stretch and the sun dips low,
The sweet sap sings, and the giggles flow.

## Threads of Citrus Hues

In vibrant threads of sunny cheer,
Citrus colors brighten the sphere.
A jester's hat, with zest so grand,
A comical fruit, we can't quite understand.

Juggling slices, a fainting stall,
A clownish peel, that slips and falls.
Giggles echo as they bounce around,
Citrus clowns perform, without a sound.

The peel unwinds, like a frisky dog,
In cartwheels bold, amid a fog.
They tease the leaves, the leaves then sway,
Nature's own jesters, come out to play.

Fruity hues merge and collide,
Crafting a mishap, they can't abide.
In this fruity tale, hearty and bright,
Laughter's key, igniting the night.

## Cascade of Sunlit Juice

A cascade flows of sunlit cheer,
Golden rivers, the end is near.
Tiny fruits splash in a playful race,
Juicy armor, no time to brace.

Squirrels dive in, with giggles abound,
Slipping and sliding, round and round.
A citrus ruckus brings smiles wide,
As laughter seeps through the countryside.

Wobbling while sipping, what a sight!
Droplets glisten in the fading light.
Every splatter, a joyful spree,
In sun-kissed juice, they feel so free.

As night draws close, with stars so bright,
Silly shadows dance with delight.
Cascading laughter in every drop,
In golden streams, the fun won't stop.

## Juxtaposition of Tart and Sweet

In the morning sun, I peel with glee,
A fruity orb, it laughs at me.
Its tartness sings, a zesty bite,
Yet sweet beneath, a pure delight.

I wrestle with this citrus foe,
It squirts and giggles, what a show!
I slice and dice, juices fly,
It's a citrus rodeo, oh my!

Each segment winks, a playful tease,
Some days it's sour, some days a breeze.
This fruit in hand, a jester's crown,
A zany taste that won't back down.

So here's to days of funny fruit,
An ode to zest, so absolute.
In kitchens bright, we dance and cheer,
With every slice, the fun is clear!

# A Mirror of Sweetness Unraveled

In the bowl, a vibrant sphere,
Reflecting laughter, bringing cheer.
Its joy is found in each bright wedge,
A citrus riddle, on the edge.

What's hidden in this sunny shell?
A sweet surprise, can you not tell?
I take a bite, my eyes go wide,
It's such a ride, I'll never hide!

The tangy dance that makes me grin,
At first it stings, then draws me in.
I wipe my face, a juicy spree,
A sticky hand, but oh, so free!

With every twist, the flavors clash,
In this wild world, I make a splash.
So here's to fruit that brings the fun,
In mirrors bright, we're never done!

## Citrus Poetry in Motion

A citrus ball, in colors bright,
Rolls on the table, what a sight!
It tumbles here, it tumbles there,
With every bounce, I can't help stare.

It speaks to me, with zestful glee,
A fruity jester, wild and free.
I take a slice, it flips, it flops,
Exploding juice, oh how it pops!

The taste, a trickster, both sour and sweet,
With every morsel, it can't be beat.
I giggle as I savor each bite,
This citrus dance, pure delight!

So let's embrace this playful treat,
In every twist, we find our beat.
A fun-filled day with juice and cheer,
The poetry of citrus is here!

## Reflections of Flora's Dusk

At twilight's touch, a citrus dream,
In shades of gold, they brightly beam.
With laughter low, they sway and spin,
In this light, the fun begins.

A tart goodbye, a sweet hello,
In motion still, they dance and flow.
Their skin's a canvas, bright and bold,
With secrets tucked in each fold.

I juggle joy with every slice,
A citrus whirlwind, oh so nice!
The evening hums a merry tune,
With fruit-filled laughter by the moon.

So here's to dusk, with flavor free,
In gardens lush, where we can see.
From sour bites to sweet embrace,
This fruity fun, our happy place!

## Depths of Bitter-Sweetness

In a bowl it sits, quite round,
A zesty orb, with secrets found.
Its bitter grin, a tasty tease,
The underdog, it aims to please.

Peeling back layers, what a sight,
Pulp like sunshine, oh what a fright!
Each slice a giggle, juicy, bright,
Who knew a fruit could cause such plight?

Sweets and sour dance a fine jig,
Life's little quirks, like a playful fig.
Lemon's jealous, for it can't compete,
With grapefruit's flair, oh so neat!

In the morning sun, it makes a stand,
A twist of fate, a zesty brand.
With every taste, here's a quip,
Even sour dreams can take a trip!

## A Tangle of Juicy Thoughts

A citrus riddle, oh what fun,
Should I share it, or just run?
Each morning slice, a giggle spree,
Why does breakfast seem so free?

Spry little wedges on my plate,
Some love it early, some just hate.
A banquet of laughs, a fruity show,
Mixing it up with every blow!

Pulp squishes out with a firm embrace,
Bursting forth, a fruity race.
Funny how it holds such zest,
For making mornings feel like jest!

So let's cheer for this jester fruit,
With every wedge, a silly hoot.
For in this tangle, we all find
Laughter dashed with citrus rind!

## The Mirage of Sunshine

I thought I'd found a sunlit friend,
A glow so bright, it won't transcend.
But in its layers lurked a bite,
A playful tease, oh what a sight!

Like mirages of joy in the dessert,
Its sweetness hides beneath the hurt.
Sip the juice, it's quite a trick,
One sip in, and you feel the kick!

Orange sun in a yellow shell,
With laughter spritzed, it casts a spell.
Suddenly, breakfast feels so grand,
In this sun's glow, we take a stand!

So here's to the mirage we adore,
Each tangy twist leaves us wanting more.
With every slice, a raucous cheer,
For citrus dreams that bring us near!

## **Citrus Collage**

Slices arranged in vibrant hues,
A citrus collage, it grants its dues.
Sours holding hands with sunny sweeps,
In the gallery of fruits, it simply leaps.

With every burst, we celebrate,
Crafting laughter, oh isn't it great?
Yellow and pink in each vivid wedge,
The perfect punch, a zesty pledge!

Each tiny segment holds a tale,
Of fruity fun, it won't derail.
This oddball fruit, a colorful muse,
Turning breakfast blues into fun cues!

So let's toast to this joyful art,
With citrus cheers, we make a start.
In every slice, a collage sings,
Of mornings bright and silly things!

## Harvested Whispers

In the garden where they dwell,
Citrus giggles, oh so swell.
Jesters in sun, they bounce and bounce,
With zesty puns that make us flounce.

Peel the laughter, squeeze the joy,
With every slice, a playful ploy.
Juice drips down, a golden flow,
A citrus clown with cheeks aglow.

Bouncing on the kitchen floor,
A fruit parade we can't ignore.
They prank us all with their bright hue,
A zany crew, it's quite the view!

As we laugh, they seem to grin,
In each bite, a playful sin.
So let the silly mood unfurl,
In this zesty, fruity world!

**Essence in Amber**

In jars of light, they twist and spin,
Sweet and tart, where do we begin?
A dance of flavors, a citrus tease,
In every bite, our worries cease.

With sticky fingers, we laugh out loud,
As juice splatters, oh, we feel proud.
The amber essence, a laughter bath,
Turning frowns into a citrus math.

They bubble and bounce with a playful touch,
These quirky fruits we love so much.
A wacky world, where smiles reign,
With every taste, a joyful gain.

So let's toast to the golden crew,
With laughter and juice, we'll break through.
In this amber haze of fun and cheer,
We'll squeeze out joy, year after year!

## Sunkissed Simplicity

The sun shines bright on zestful skin,
With every grin, the laughter spins.
Wobbling on the kitchen rack,
These sunny orbs never lack.

They roll about, a fruity game,
Each little squish calls out a name.
A pucker here, a joke or two,
In this fruit bowl, giggles brew.

Chopping slices, what a sight,
Juice squirts out with sheer delight.
A citrus pie, or maybe cake,
With every flavor, our bakes awake!

So here's to fun in every bite,
With teasing sweetness, oh what a sight!
In sunnier days, we sense their glow,
Life's simple joys, we gladly show!

## The Luminescent Sphere

In daylight's glow, they shine so bright,
Orbiting laughter, pure delight.
Spheres of sunshine roll and play,
Chasing shadows, brightening the day.

With jokes on peels, they tease our minds,
In every squeeze, giggles we find.
A fruity jest, a zesty thrill,
They keep us laughing, what a skill!

Slice and dice, the flavors burst,
In this juicy world, we're always versed.
With each tangy taste, we cheer and sing,
Life's shining fruit, our revelry brings.

So raise a glass, let's toast the fun,
To these bright orbs, let laughter run.
In the glow of joy, we'll dance and cheer,
For every moment shared is dear!

## Yonder Fruity Glimmer

In the grove where sunshine plays,
A silly fruit begins to sway,
Its roundness boasts a bouncy cheer,
In citrus worlds, it's king this year.

With zest that tickles all around,
The bright orb rolls upon the ground,
It laughs aloud, it dances free,
A jester in the tree-topped spree.

Orange and yellow, a bright parade,
Juggling joy in every shade,
The taste of summer, pure delight,
It bounces back with all its might.

"Catch me if you can!" it shouts,
As silly squirrels all dance about,
A fruity prankster on the run,
Its playful antics, so much fun!

## Essence of Citrus Serenity

Amidst the leaves, a vibrant gleam,
A citrine orb, it starts to beam,
With laughter sweet, it holds a throne,
In citrus realms it feels at home.

It giggles as the sunlight shines,
With every flicker of the vines,
A splash of wit, a dash of flair,
Its juicy grin beyond compare.

The blossoms tease with scents so bright,
While playful breezes take to flight,
It jests and tumbles, spins with glee,
The essence of hilarity.

"Try to peel me!" it dares, so sly,
But slippery skins make laughter fly,
Unruly zest that stirs the joy,
In nature's circus, it's the ploy.

## The Dance of Sweetness

A twirl of zest amid the leaves,
A citrus star that never grieves,
It spins and hops with such delight,
In sunshine's glow, it feels just right.

With every swirl, it shimmies wide,
Beneath the tree where dreams abide,
A fruity jig, a zestful romp,
In nature's dance, it helps us chomp.

It frolics 'round with fruity friends,
A merry troupe that never ends,
Together they frolic in the sun,
A citrus party, oh what fun!

So raise a toast, come join the beat,
In harmony, it's oh so sweet,
Here's to the joy of their ballet,
A fruity dance that steals the day!

## Harvesting Light

In orchards bright with sun-kissed cheer,
A ball of joy, so round and dear,
It lights the branches, oh so bold,
A treasure wrapped in warmth of gold.

Picking laughter from the trees,
With every pluck, it swings with ease,
A cheerful shout, "I'm ripe and fine!"
This citrus queen loves to shine.

With playful giggles, it rolls and plays,
Through grassy fields on sunny days,
A bounty sweet, a burst of fun,
Harvesting light, its work is done.

So gather round, let laughter grow,
As tangy tales begin to flow,
In every slice, a smile so bright,
In fruity realms, we find delight.

## **Ripe Reflections**

In a mirror of zest, it grins wide,
Belly full of sunshine, it can't hide.
The breakfast table chuckles in cheer,
As juice drips like laughter, oh so near.

Sliced and shiny, it wears a crown,
A citrus ball, never a frown.
With each juicy bite, a giggle may burst,
It's a morning delight, bubble-filled first.

Fruits in a bowl, having a ball,
The sweetness and tartness, that's the call.
As we fork and we spoon, it winks with glee,
A taste of pure joy, as funny as can be.

In lunchtime's limelight, it won't fade,
With salad and sandwiches, it's always played.
One quick bite, and the world's a fun ride,
In the land of the tangy, it's where we reside.

## The Peel's Secret

Behind that bright skin, a tale unfolds,
Of zest and of pith, and laughter untold.
Peel it away, and what do we find?
A world of sweet giggles, flavors entwined.

Each layer reveals a juicy surprise,
A citrus comedian in disguise.
With rolling laughter as you take a bite,
Life feels so silly, everything's bright.

Split open the sections, they pop with cheer,
Like tiny sun drops, oh so dear.
It's wobbly and jiggly, like friends at play,
In the kitchen's bright light, they dance and sway.

So gather your spoons, let's have some fun,
With this fruity jester, we'll never be done.
She shares all her secrets, with smiles and zest,
In the realm of the citrus, we're surely the best.

## Light Dancing on Citrus

Sunlight bounces off surfaces round,
A citrus fiesta, joy can be found.
Each wedge takes a bow, each segment a dance,
In the spotlight of morning, they twirl and prance.

The tangy aroma fills up the air,
A zesty partner, oh how we share.
With laughter a'plenty, in every bite,
Taste buds rejoicing, a true delight.

Glints of bright orange, peeking through green,
Creating a scene like none ever seen.
Fun flavors collide in this merry parade,
With giggles and glimmers, no worries invade.

So join in the joy, let's savor the light,
A citrus celebration, pure and bright.
In every slice, there's magic to find,
With zest and with laughter, our hearts unwind.

## Haiku of a Tangy Morning

Morning whispers sweet,
A slice of sunshine awaits,
Citrus dreams take flight.

Honeyed laughter sings,
Juicy bursts of joy collide,
Nature's joke unpeels.

Zesty smiles abound,
In each tangy orb of gold,
A giggle revealed.

## **A Fateful Twist of Peel**

Once upon a fruit parade,
A citrus clown just couldn't fade.
With every twist, a sour grin,
A peel that danced, a comedy win.

In the sun, it slipped and slid,
Echoing laughs, a playful bid.
It rolled away, a zany plot,
The juiciest jester ever sought.

All the slices cheered for more,
As it bounced off the kitchen floor.
In a bowl, it took a dive,
In citrus chaos, we felt alive!

So here's a joke, just try to catch,
The funniest fruit with a playful scratch.
Twist your fate, let out a squeal,
In laughter's zest, we all can heal.

## Pool of Citrus Epiphanies

Gazing deep in a bowl divine,
A round, bright orb began to shine.
In its depths, a secret swam,
What if grapefruit drinks with jam?

It pondered life with zestful flair,
What's laughter without a juicy dare?
Sipping nectar, it wore a grin,
No better way to begin to spin.

Bouncing thoughts in a citrus dream,
Do fruit salads like to scheme?
Mixing flavors, a playful debate,
When's the last time you danced on a plate?

So gather fruits, both round and square,
Join this pool; there's laughs to share.
Life's too short for bitter meals,
Let giggles burst with citrus peels!

## Slices of Summer Reminiscence

Ah, summers spent with rays of gold,
Among the trees, stories unfold.
Eating slices, sweet and bold,
Each bite was magic, or so we're told.

With every wedge, a giggle popped,
As juice flew high and laughter topped.
Who knew a citrus could inspire
The wildest games of jest and fire?

Remember when we squeezed and squirted?
The serious faces that we flirted?
Up in the air, a wedge took flight,
Landing smack on our neighbor's kite.

So cheers to juicy, silly days,
Where friendly battles ignited rays.
In slices true, our joy shall sprout,
Summer memories never in doubt!

## Pools of Amber Delight

In a bowl of amber sheen,
A curious fruit caught my keen.
With a wink and a twist of peel,
It promised tales that felt so real.

It pooled in laughter, reflections bright,
Each citrus chuckle a pure delight.
Domestic life turned into a show,
As jokes flowed like a steady flow.

"Is it too tart?" I asked in jest,
"Nope!" it chirped, "you're quite the guest!"
With every sip, a comic twist,
Life served funny in a citrus mist.

So raise your glasses, take a chance,
Let flavor lead you to a dance.
In pools of sun and laughter sweet,
Embrace the joy—oh, what a treat!

## Ripples of Flavor and Light

In the bowl, a bright orb found,
A dance of zest, with laughs unbound.
Sliced in half, a citrus grin,
Juice spills forth, let the fun begin!

Pithy jokes between each bite,
Witty comments, oh what a sight!
Sticky fingers, giggles soar,
Who knew fruit could be such a chore?

Rolling round, an eager tease,
Citrus smiles put minds at ease.
Squeeze the day from dawn till night,
With a twist, everything feels right!

Mirth and cheer in every slice,
Juicy puns, oh how nice!
Sunshine laughter, we'll toast away,
A fruity feast, come what may!

## Threads of Citrus Whimsy

Citrus threads weave tales so bright,
A tapestry of tasty delight.
Each segment bursting with surprise,
Witty tales meet sunny skies.

Who knew tang could spark such glee?
Witty banter, just you and me.
Peel away those worries tight,
Let's frolic in this fruity light!

A zesty giggle, orange and pink,
Slips from our lips before we think.
Twirl the zest, throw back some cheer,
Citrus whimsy draws us near!

Fragrant joy drapes every scene,
In this carnival of the green.
With each bite, a chuckle flows,
Oh, the fun that citrus knows!

## **Seasons of Citrus Echo**

In spring, a burst of sunny cheer,
Lemons laugh, "Let's make it clear!"
Summer's zest, a tangy shout,
Invite the friends, let's twist about!

Autumn brings a citrus fling,
Harvesting joy, oh what a thing!
Winter's chill, a lemonade glow,
Hot cups brewing, laughter in tow!

Each season whispers, "Have some fun!"
Squeeze it in, let's all run!
With every drop, the smiles grow,
Echoes of joy in citrus flow!

So let us dance, let puckers play,
In a world where fruit's the way.
With laughter bright, we'll toast away,
To every citrus holiday!

## Aroma of a Sunkissed Day

With aromas bright, the sun's delight,
Citrus dreams in morning light.
Zesty wafts fill the air,
Laughter bubbles everywhere!

A breakfast feast with colors bold,
Every slice, a story told.
Sweet and sour, mix with glee,
In this citrus symphony!

Smiles awaken with each bite,
Under sunshine, feeling right.
Squeezed in joy, a jolly cheer,
Sunkissed moments through the year!

Let's raise a glass, do a jig,
Juicy quotes, let's laugh big!
In the essence of this day,
The fruits of laughter lead the way!

# Honeyed Twilight Reflections

In the twilight glow, joy takes flight,
A zesty orb spins, what a silly sight.
Juice drips like laughter, so sweet and bright,
As shadows dance, chasing day into night.

A peel so peachy, it grins just right,
Hiding secrets, oh what a playful byte!
With every glimmer, it'll take a bite,
What antics await in this fruity light!

Rolling down hills, a citrusy spree,
Chasing the sunset, so wild and free.
Lemons laugh loudly, just wait and see,
In honeyed twilight, it's pure jubilee.

A silly parade of flavors, oh my!
Orange giggles as the day waves goodbye.
With every sip, the humor won't die,
As night wraps around, this fruit won't lie.

## The Light that Drips


A splash of sunshine, drops of fun,
Citrus giggles dance on the run.
Each droplet winks, it's never done,
Even the clouds join; they're easily won.

Rays of mischief, they drip and sway,
Caught in a bottle, the juice will play.
Sipping the laughter, in a sweet ballet,
It's a tangy carnival, hip-hip-hooray!

The shadows stretch, but what a sight,
Lemonade dreams bubble up, so bright.
Citrus confetti swirls with delight,
In this sweet chaos, everything feels right.

So raise a glass, let the giggles flow,
A liquid laugh, come and join the show.
With every sip, let the humor grow,
The light that drips, steals the whole tableau.

## Citrus Secrets unfurling

Hidden behind a cheeky skin,
Lies a world of fun where jokes begin.
Citrus mysteries, oh what a spin,
Unravel the laughter, let the games win.

Peel back the layers, what do we find?
Silly whispers of the sweetest kind.
Tickled by tang, the mind's intertwined,
In this fruity laughter, we're all aligned.

With each zesty burst, the giggles spring,
Juggling juiciness, oh how we swing.
Lime and orange, join in and sing,
Citrus secrets can't help but bling.

Bursting with sunshine, bursting with cheer,
Fruity companions, drawing us near.
In every sip, we'll have no fear,
Citrus secrets unfurl, year after year.

## Corner of Citrus Dreams

In a corner where citrus dreams thrive,
Lemons laugh loudly, keeping hopes alive.
Orange whispers tickle, jovial and spry,
It's a zesty kingdom, oh my, oh my!

Crammed with sweetness, this nook of fun,
Mirthful mandarins dance 'til they're done.
Grapefruits giggle, giving joy on the run,
Sunshine and humor, for everyone!

As flavors collide in this vibrant space,
Each bite's a chuckle, a fruity embrace.
With laughter lingering, they quicken the pace,
In this citrus carnival, we set our place.

So come one, come all to the dreamiest spot,
Where laughter and joy are served piping hot.
In the corner of dreams, let's tie the knot,
Citrus delight, here happiness is caught!

## **Aromatic Illusions**

In the fruit bowl, a bright orb shines,
Its scent dances in zigzag lines.
A slice of laughter on breakfast plates,
Where juiciness meets hilarious fates.

Zesty giggles burst from the peel,
A shimmer of joy is the real deal.
Each bite sparks a chuckle, so sweet,
Who knew breakfast could be this neat?

**The Glint of Zest**

Lemon and orange hold hands with glee,
But there's one fruit laughing, come see!
With its bright skin and quirky grin,
It knows it's the funniest within.

Peeling back layers, a comedy show,
Each segment struts with a vibrant glow.
Juice flies like jokes in the air,
Citrus theater, a zestful affair.

## Fragrant Echoes in Water

A splash of color in the glass,
Bubbles bounce, time flies fast.
Echoes of giggles, a tangy tune,
As the shimmering drink captures the moon.

Sips of laughter in each tiny drop,
A fruity party that won't ever stop.
With every twist, a wink and a cheer,
This drink's got humor, oh dear, oh dear!

## Chasing Sunbeams

Under bright skies, we skip and sway,
With fragrant friends, we play all day.
Chasing sunbeams, we giggle and run,
  This fruity game is all about fun.

Laughter bursts like seeds in the air,
Each sunny moment, a joyful flare.
With zany grins and twinkling eyes,
  Friendship's zest is a sweet surprise.

## The Pulse of Tangy Euphoria

In a bowl of sunshine, it sits quite bold,
A citrus ball of joy, with stories untold.
It wobbles and jiggles, a jester of zest,
With each little slice, our taste buds are blessed.

Sugar and spice in a sweet tango dance,
With pithy wisdom, they take a chance.
A burst of delight, a splish and a splash,
The wacky rhythms of flavor clash!

Peeling the layers, it giggles and grins,
A circus of citrus, where laughter begins.
Sour and sweet in a playful affair,
Its cheeky demeanor, we can't help but share.

So seize the moment, don't let it slip,
Join in the fun, with a zesty quip.
A pulse of tangy joy, forever we seek,
In this merry madness, let's play hide and seek!

## **Evocative Citrus Dreams**

In dreams of sunsets and bright citrus glow,
A round little muse, with a delightful show.
Each segment a giggle, a splash in the night,
A fruit that knows how to bring pure delight.

With neon yellow smiles, it rolls on the floor,
Bouncing through laughter, a zest we adore.
In a bowl of cheer, it whispers and beams,
Tickling our senses with fruity dreams.

A dance of the taste buds, a carnival feast,
Where tangy trolls laugh, and sweetness released.
It winks from the counter, a chubby delight,
With jokes in the aroma, oh what a sight!

So let's raise a glass to this citrusy fun,
Where dreams all collide and the laughter's begun.
In every bright axle of orange and cheer,
We savor this fruit; its news—loud and clear!

## **Delicate Veil of Juice**

Beneath a bright skin, a treasure awaits,
With a laugh and a splash that dances like fates.
It spills out its secrets in glimmers and glows,
A delicate veil of what nature bestows.

A jiggle, a wobble, it teases and sways,
With sweetness that sings through the sunniest days.
From breakfast to brunch, a whimsical muse,
In the apéritif hours, it's hard to refuse.

Citrusy giggles in every dear drop,
Tales of tangy wonder that never will stop.
Its laughter bursts forth in a joyful parade,
A playful reminder that joy's never delayed.

So let us give cheers to this gleeful delight,
In a world full of sweetness, it shines oh so bright.
With each little sip, let the giggles ensue,
As we savor the joy of this delicate hue!

## **Pale Crimson Revelations**

Underneath the moonlight, a secret unfolds,
With a wink of the rind, a story retold.
The blush on its belly makes everyone glee,
A playful reminder of the fruit's jubilee.

In bowls of bright laughter, the ruby does dance,
Eliciting giggles with every sweet glance.
A sip of the evening, a burst of sheer bliss,
In pale crimson wonder, we find our sweet kiss.

Each bite is a surprise, a party of zest,
A fruit with a flair that knows how to jest.
It leaps from the table with zestful allure,
Making our taste buds feel ever so pure.

So join in the mischief, let's laugh and rejoice,
With pale crimson revelations, we give it a voice.
In a world full of sweetness, let's share the delight,
As we dance with our fruit under starry night!

www.ingramcontent.com/pod-product-compliance
Lightning Source LLC
Chambersburg PA
CBHW060122230426
43661CB00003B/296